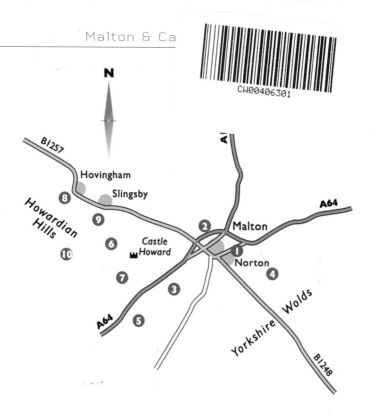

Contents

WALK 1: Derventio, Malton Priory & Eden Camp

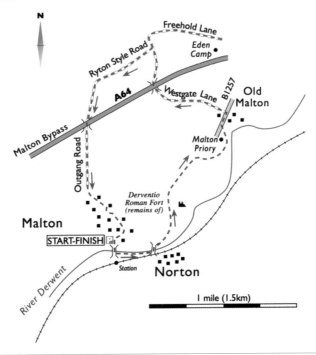

Distance: 4 miles (6 km).
Time: 2 hours plus time to explore Malton Priory & Eden Camp.
Start/finish: Malton Bridge (grid ref 787715).
Parking: Water Lane long stay car park off Railway Road.
Terrain: Easy. Field paths and tracks, then street walking.
Public transport: Leeds-York-Scarborough TransPennine train services stop at Malton, as do Coastliner 843 bus services from York and Scarborough.
Refreshments/facilities: Excellent choices of cafés and pubs in Malton; café at Eden Camp Visitor Centre. Toilets at Malton Bus Station and town centre; also in Eden Camp.

An easy walk through the outskirts of Malton to discover the site of a Roman Camp and, in nearby Old Malton, a priory church that once belonged to a unique English order of canons. There's also the option of visiting the remarkable Eden Camp (an additional 20 minutes' walk each way).

WALKS AROUND
Malton & Castle Howard

Ten great walks of between 4 and 6 miles

Colin Speakman

Dalesman

Introduction

Malton is a small but vibrant town in Ryedale, noted for its celebrated food market and food festivals (market day Saturday) and for racehorse breeding. The town lies north of the River Derwent, but south of the river is its twin, Norton (Malton Railway and Bus Stations are actually in Norton). To complicate matters even further, the village of Old Malton is less than a mile away. However, Malton and its medieval church, 18th-century former town hall, attractive shops and market place, is the focal point.

Malton as a town dates back to the first century when the Roman fort of Derventio and its adjacent civil settlement were established on the banks of the Derwent. The small Malton Museum, now in the Parish Rooms in Yorkersgate, contains many Roman and medieval remains from the fort and nearby excavations.

The town continued to prosper from medieval times as an inland port at the highest navigable point on the Derwent, situated below its confluence with the Rye and above the spectacular Derwent Gorge, which separates the Howardian Hills from the Wolds. For the walker, good transport links (mercifully the town is bypassed by the A64) and superb countryside close by makes the town an excellent base to explore both the nearby Yorkshire Wolds that overlook the town and the Howardian Hills Area of Outstanding Natural Beauty.

This magnificent area of 79 square miles of predominantly Jurassic limestone countryside, with its scattered areas of woodland and pasture, takes its name from the Howard family. Castle Howard estate has over several centuries been carefully landscaped, as have neighbouring estates, as much for sporting interest, including pheasant shooting, as agriculture. What makes this landscape unique is not only the dominance of one of England's greatest country houses, designed by John Vanbrugh (1664-1726), but the estate itself. Carefully positioned architectural features and follies are placed in prominent locations to replicate the magical beauty of a 17th-century painting by Salvator Rosa or Claude Lorraine.

Even on these short walks, paths can be steep and muddy. Boots are advised for all walks, and rainwear and emergency food and drink should always be carried. Have a good map with you. Highly recommended is OS Explorer 300 Howardian Hills & Malton which covers everything in this book. Walks 2 and 5 cross between the West and East sides of the map. Most paths, thanks to Howardian Hills AONB staff and local Ramblers, are well signed and waymarked and in good order. Take all litter home with you, close gates (unless clearly propped open) and keep dogs on the lead at all times – there are almost always sheep or cattle about. Take special care when crossing the many busy roads in the area.

For local bus information (all walks are, at time of writing, accessible by public transport) contact the local operator, Stephensons of Easingwold, on 01347 838990, or visit their website www.stephensonsofeasingwold.co.uk

From the south, railway station side of Malton Bridge, take the footpath through a small gate down steps alongside the River Derwent, signed Centenary Way. This flagged riverside walk leads behind the bus station and industrial buildings into a small riverside park, to emerge on Norton Road near the level crossing. Turn left over the river bridge. Cross at the pedestrian gap into Castlegate, then take the first road right, Sheepfoot Hill, soon passing the Fire Station.

Near the end of the lane (792716), take the path (signed) left into an open field. Where it forks take the path half right (not signed) which leads across rough grassland.

Various interpretive boards in this open area indicate the site of the civil settlement that formed part of the Roman fort of Derventio, and behind that, above an embankment, the site of the fort itself. Many finds from here are kept in Malton Museum.

Follow the path to a pedestrian gate which leads across the tree-lined trackbed of the long-vanished Malton-Thirsk railway line. Continue to the Old Malton Road. Turn right here, following the surfaced path inside the hedge. This goes along the field edge and road for around a quarter of a mile towards Old Malton. Turn right where the housing begins and go alongside the playing field for 100 yards. Ignore the wooden sign for a permissive path directly ahead, but bear left on the right-of-way which runs alongside a hedge. At a junction of paths keep bearing slightly left alongside the

tall hedge towards the church. You emerge in a surfaced track at the yard and rear entrance of St Mary's Priory Church. Go through the stone arch on your left which leads through the churchyard to the main church entrance.

Take time to explore this lovely, if much restored building, with its massive Early English columns and decorative features. The church once belonged to the remarkable 12th-century Gilbertine priory of canons, an unusual and exclusively English order of 26 Houses, an order of (strictly separated) both canons and nuns. There is a small collection of medieval artefacts inside the church, including the head of an Anglo-Viking cross, and interpretive boards telling the history of the church and the Gilbertine Order.

From the church entrance return to the drive, head to the main road and turn right for 350 yards. Turn left at the

Meadow pipit

Wentworth Arms, along Westgate, a quiet lane with attractive pantiled and thatched cottages. Follow the main track which eventually bears right at Rainbow Equine Centre to the elevated bridge over the A64 Malton bypass. Keep ahead for a quarter mile to where a track, Ryton Style Road, leads off left. If you are going to Eden Camp continue in the same direction for 120 yards. Turn right along a tree-lined track, Freehold Lane. Where this reaches Edenhouse Road, turn right past the tractor depot to the entrance to Eden Camp.

This former Prisoner of War camp, situated in the actual huts used by Italian and German prisoners in the 1940s, is now a Museum of Modern History. Displays deal with two major world wars – exhibits include amazingly realistic animations of both trench warfare and the Blitz, and the impacts of both wars on civilian life. Other major military campaigns fought by British troops in the 20th century are also recalled. There is a café, bar and shop. Open daily – www.edencamp.co.uk tel: 01653 69777.

From Eden Camp return the same way to the junction with Ryton Style Road. Head down this pleasant farm access track past open fields to its junction with another track known as Cheapside Road. Turn left to pass more open fields. Ascend past another junction of paths, to Outgang Road. This unsurfaced track leads to the second bridge over the A64. Continue over the brow of the hill to meet busy Pasture Road. Turn right to the traffic lights. Cross and turn left into Newbiggin and follow the pavement down into the centre of Malton.

Watch for rabbits playing in the pastures

CMI

WALK 2: Ryedale villages — Broughton & Swinton

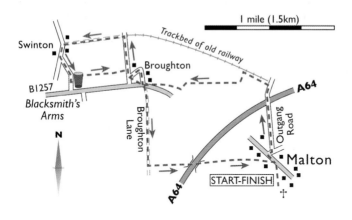

Distance: 6 miles (9.5 km). Time: 3 hours.
Terrain: Easy; tracks, field paths and quiet suburban roads.
Start/finish: Malton Market Place by Parish Church (grid ref 785717).
Parking: Long stay parking in Malton: Water Lane (off Railway Street)
and in Wentworth Street.
Refreshments/facilities: Blacksmiths Arms in Swinton; choice of pubs,
cafés, in Malton. Toilets at Malton Market Place or Bus Station.
Public transport: Trans Pennine Trains from York and Scarborough to
Malton Station, Coastline Bus services 843. Walk can be shortened to 2 or 3
miles by catching return 194 Malton-Hovingham bus (not Sundays) from either
Swinton or Broughton at bus stops on main road.

This pleasant walk takes you on the edge of Malton and the Howardian Hills to two of the villages along the ancient line of freshwater springs below the Howardian Hills. It makes use of footbridges over the busy Malton bypass to follow footpaths through arable fields and pasture. There is also an intriguing section of trackbed, the relic of a long-forgotten country railway which once carried regular steam trains between Malton, Hovingham and Thirsk.

From the market place, turn north to cross to the Golden Lion hotel and into the Shambles, a pedestrian street. Cross Victoria Road straight ahead by the Spotted Cow pub, and go up Mount Road. At the end, turn right into The Mount, an attractive road of Victorian houses. Follow this down to where it joins Middlecave Road. Keep ahead along Mount Crescent down to the busy junction and traffic lights on Newbiggin. Cross, turning right into Pasture Road. Almost immediately, by a small electric substation, turn left into a cindery track, signed Bridleway. This is Outgang Road.

Follow it due north, between new housing, and then across open pastureland to where the track crosses the Malton bypass. Descend gently for 150 yards to where, just before a house (784729), a wooden sign indicates a path along a grassy verge by a stretch of scrubland.

This trackbed and rotting bits of fence are all that remain of the Thirsk and Malton Railway which ran between Malton and Pilmoor south of Thirsk, on what is now the East Coast main line, connecting several Ryedale villages. The single-track line was opened in 1853 with stations at Amotherby, Barton-le-Street and Hovingham. It closed to passengers in 1930 and as a freight branch in 1964.

The path follows the old railway for two fields, before turning sharp left at a tall hawthorn hedge. The path and hedge zigzag right and left before finally meeting a broader bridleway, Crabtree Lane (780730).

Turn right along a broad, green way defined by wheel tracks, across two fields under pylon wires. At the third field, by a hedge and two trees, though the right of way goes left across the field (Chapel Garth), most walkers follow the field edge to the left corner. Then go right, to a bridle gate 100 yards from the field corner. Through the gate go diagonally right along a clear grassy path, which heads towards trees and another bridle gate. Turn right, through a field gate, into a long narrow field behind houses, to the edge Broughton.

Turn right, into the village centre – mainly modern housing. Though there is a short cut to the top of the village, it is partly blocked, and most walkers will find it easier to turn left into Beach Croft Lane, bearing left until you join Moor Lane, in the older part of the village. Turn right, passing cottages. Head due north through and out of the village.

Where the lane ends by Gate House, take the path left signed Swinton, which once again follows the old railway trackbed. This becomes a farm track which joins Low Lane north of Swinton.

Turn left here. When you reach the fork in the road, turn left along East Lane through this pleasant village. Pass Low Farm, and follow the raised pavement

Malton sign, along another enclosed and well used path (which can be muddy in winter). This leads to another crossing of paths. Keep directly ahead with the Malton signs to soon reach and cross the bypass along an elegant footbridge.

Turn left at the path end, and then bear right along a broad track which leads into the end of Middlecave Lane. Pick up the direct route along the pavement, past Malton School, to the centre of Malton.

above the lane. Unless you are heading for the welcoming Blacksmiths Arms, at the lane corner on the B1257 road, look for a track entrance on the left by a cottage with a wooden sign indicating Broughton.

Where this track bends right, a pedestrian gate leads to a path enclosed between wire fences. This turns left, then right, outside the perimeter of two fields. It then crosses two more open fields before reaching Broughton again. Turn right here. Look for a stile on the left in the hedge just past a brick farm building. The way crosses the field to another stile into the path alongside the B1257.

Go left here, but cross the main road opposite the lay-by to reach Broughton Lane on the right. The pleasant farm track and bridleway soon becomes a green way, gently climbing. At the crossing of paths, turn left. Follow the

Facing page, a stoat; above left, greater woodrush; above, monkey flower

9

Walk 3 – Along the Derwent

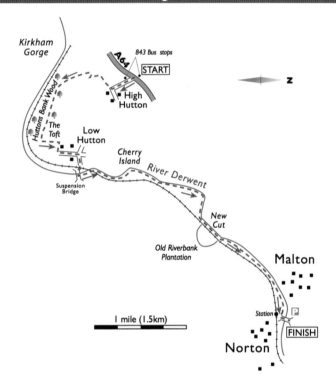

Distance: 5½ miles (9 km). Time: 2½ hours.
Terrain: Easy – tracks and riverside paths. Several stiles. This walk should not be attempted if the River Derwent is in flood or is exceptionally high, as riverside paths can flood dangerously.
Start: Hutton Lane End lay-by and bus stop (grid ref 750687).
Finish: Malton Bridge (linear walk).
Parking: Centre of Malton (Long stay car park at Water Lane, by Malton Bridge) then catch a (frequent) Coastliner 843 bus from the Bus station towards York to Hutton Lane End, walking back to parked vehicle.
Refreshments/facilities: Malton – choice of cafés, inns, shops.
Toilets at bus station or in town centre.
Public transport: Coastliner bus service 843 from Leeds, York, Malton Scarborough. Alight at Hutton Lane Ends, return from Malton Bus Station.
TransPennine Train to Malton then Coastliner 843 as above.

A walk which starts near two attractive villages situated on a plateau above Kirkham Gorge, then follows the River Derwent and the York-Scarborough railway line into the heart of the town.

Alight from the York-bound Coastliner at the bus stop by the lay-by just past the lane end to High and Low Hutton. If alighting from a Malton-bound bus, cross the A64 carefully at the refuge to the High Hutton Lane end. Follow the lane towards High Hutton past the rear of High Hutton Hall, ignoring the first path to the right.

Where Back Lane turns sharp left towards High Hutton, take the footpath sharp right signed St Andrew's Lane. This goes along the field edge by a hedge and through another gate. There are fine views across the valley towards the Wolds. After 300 yards turn left past an ash tree (749682). The path is now at the far side of the hedge, again signed St Andrew's Lane.

When you reach St Andrew's Lane, a green track, turn right here for 100 yards to the next junction. Take the path on the left, now signed for Low Hutton village. This path follows the top of the escarpment, with intriguing views through the trees into the steep valley of the River Derwent, Kirkham Gorge.

This remarkable natural feature was created after the last Ice Age some 12,000 years ago when glacial waters, trapped in what is now the Vale of Pickering, created a huge natural lake. The waters were eventually to escape southwards via Kirkham (see Walk 5) gouging out this twisting, steep sided gorge in the process.

Continue past the edge of several large arable fields named Annan Field and The Tofts, divided by hedges with stiles and kissing gates. The path gradually curves to the east before at The Tofts turning sharp left along the hedge towards Low Hutton. The path turns right where it reaches the edge of the village gardens. Go left to join the end of the main street into this pretty village.

Walk to the village green and the small war memorial before bearing right past the No Through Road sign down towards the river. Bear right as you near the riverside to cross the steel suspension bridge.

Now follow the Centenary Way signs sharp left down to the riverside. Walk upstream through dense vegetation and woodland. The path soon goes under a bridge carrying the York-Scarborough railway line, and follows an attractive but slightly unnervingly narrow route on the riverbank between river and railway. Turn back at this point if the river is high.

The River Derwent, one of Yorkshire's most important rivers, runs for 72 miles from near Fylingdales on the North York Moors

Cottongrass

to where it joins the River Ouse at Barmby-on-the-Marsh. Once important for navigation and commerce, serving several towns as far upstream as Malton, the Derwent remains a vital source of water supply for several major towns and cities, as well as having many leisure uses and retaining high value for nature conservation. But it is also notorious for flooding as recently built flood defences will testify.

The path opens out into pasture. You soon pass Cherry Islands, a series of inlets used for leisure boats. Now follows a long stretch of pleasant riverside path, marked by occasional gates and stiles. The path heads north to where river and railway again squeeze their way into a very narrow corridor dense with riverbank vegetation.

This artificial section of straightened river, known as New Cut, was created to avoid building extra bridges on the York to Scarborough railway line. Amazing as it now seems, this line was built entirely with manual labour, in just a year, during 1844/45. The abandoned section of river now forms a crescent-shaped series of ornamental ponds to the east of the line.

River and footpath now swing clear of the railway, passing an industrial park on the other side of the river on the outskirts of Malton. It then meets houses overlooking the river, some in quite grand style, before reaching flood defences, a playground and homes by Malton Bridge. Turn left across the bridge to the town centre for refreshment and the main car parks, or right for the bus and rail stations.

Grey wagtail

Walk 4 – Settrington and North Grimston

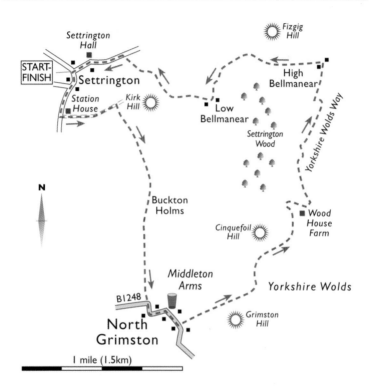

Settrington Hall

START-FINISH
Settrington

Station House

Kirk Hill

Fizgig Hill

High Bellmanear

Low Bellmanear

Settrington Wood

Yorkshire Wolds Way

N

Buckton Holms

Cinquefoil Hill

Wood House Farm

Middleton Arms

B1248

North Grimston

Yorkshire Wolds

Grimston Hill

1 mile (1.5km)

Distance: 6 miles (10 km). **Time:** 3 hours.
Terrain: Moderate – tracks and field paths, one steep climb, several stiles.
Start & finish: Settrington Village (grid ref 837701).
Parking: On road, by the broad verge south of village (837701); or at the village hall – £2, please make payment as requested.
(This extends the walk by one mile.)
Refreshments/facilities: Middleton Arms, North Grimston. Toilets: Middleton Arms (patrons only); Malton.
Public transport: Stephensons 190 from Malton – alight in village centre or at cross roads south of the village. Limited service – not Sundays (on return journey option of 4 mile level walk through fields along Centenary Way from Settrington back to Malton via Norton).

A walk through the northern edge of the Yorkshire Wolds, including a short section of the Yorkshire Wolds Way, enjoying some characteristic chalkland scenery, steep escarpments, dry grassy valley bottoms and some magnificent views.

Settrington, where the walk starts, is a pretty village, well worth exploring, with an extended village green along Settrington Beck, crossed by pretty fords and footbridges. It is very much an estate village dominated by the fine Georgian Settrington House (no public access) and handsome church. Most of the walk is on land owned by the Settrington estate. Please keep dogs on leads.

From the end of the village, walk due south on the road towards North Grimston. About 200 yards past the junction with the Malton road turn left at the old station house along the stony track to Kirk Hill Farm.

Station House is a reminder of the existence of the long-vanished railway through the heart of the Yorkshire Wolds, linking Malton with Driffield. Opened in 1853, it closed to passengers in 1950 and freight in 1958. Its daily passenger train chugging along the deep chalk cuttings was known as the

Siskin

Malton Dodger. Note the abandoned cutting on the right.

Follow the farm access road as it dips and crosses Settrington Beck. At the farmhouse, turn sharp right to the pedestrian gate (waymarked). Ten yards past the gate, bear right to a narrow wooden bridge over the stream. The narrow but distinct path (waymarked) follows the winding stream through open pasture with mature trees. You reach a small woodland with an overgrown pond at Buckton Holms, entered and exited by a stile and a gate. Keep to the field side, right, to head straight towards Bellmanear Farm.

Keep to the right of the beck behind the farm, over stiles to the farm access track (843683). Take the stile on the left to access the adjacent field. Turn right alongside the wire fence to the next stile. Maintain the same direction towards a ruined cottage ahead. Beyond this, stone

Field vole

steps on the right lead into a short lane past North Grimston House into the village. North Grimston is a charming village, albeit on the busy B1248 road, with a village green, stream, benches and the welcoming Middleton Arms.

Continue beyond the inn and head uphill, taking care with traffic where the pavement ends. At the entrance to a broad track (845675) with cattle grid, turn left. This becomes a pleasant green lane below the chalk escarpment of Grimston, with increasingly fine views to your left. The track descends to cross a shallow valley formed by Whitestone Beck before climbing sharply up Cinquefoil Hill. It then joins the Yorkshire Wolds Way National Trail south of Wood House Farm. Follow the Wolds Way as it climbs past the farm, with its handsome brick arched stables. Turn left at the sharp bend to head up to the edge of Settrington Wood, a large plantation.

The Wolds Way bears right then left around the wood edge (follow the waymarks). Where the track splits, the main one bearing right, look for the acorn waymarked narrow path leading to the right, just inside the wood and parallel to the track. This swings north-eastwards but after quarter of a mile, turns left with clear Wolds Way signs to the far side of the plantation. Turn right to ascend the ridge.

From here are superb views across to Malton, the Howardian Hills and North York Moors. In the distance is the Vale of York and Pennines beyond.

After 350 yards, turn left at the footpath sign and stile. The path heads due west,

Cranesbill

gently descending along the field edge to a gate and stile into a wood. Keep the same direction to the next stile. The path now curves to the right over rough pasture, Fizgig Hill. Look for the small waymark halfway down which directs the walker to the path down to the gate below left. Go through here then straight ahead over wet pasture towards Low Bellmanear Farm.

Turn right as you reach the drive west of the farmhouse. Follow this drive as it ascends past a wood, and then up to the lane. Turn left. Descend past the entrance to Settrington House to the edge of Settrington village where you began the walk.

Walk 5 – Kirkham Priory and Gorge

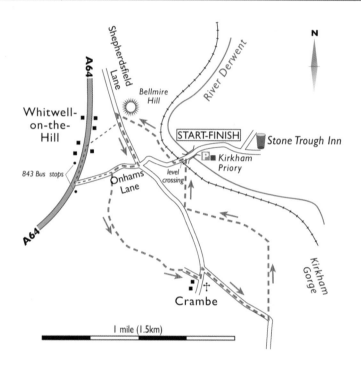

Distance: 4 miles (6 km). Time: 2 hours.
Terrain: Moderate – field paths and lanes. Two steep climbs.
Start & Finish: Kirkham Priory (grid ref 735658).
Parking: Kirkham Priory car park (free). Can be busy at summer weekends.
Refreshments/facilities: Stone Trough Inn (450 yards uphill east of Kirkham Priory); small shop with coffee machine in priory. Toilets at Kirkham Priory or Stone Trough Inn (customers only). Picnic area within priory grounds.
Public transport: Coastliner service 843 between York and Malton. Alight at Whitwell-on-the-Hill summit, and take Onhams Lane (brown sign to Kirkham Priory). If coming from York or returning to Malton use the refuge point with good sightlines some 20 yards north east of Malton-bound bus stop to cross the A64 safely – beware very fast traffic. Join the walk at Onhams Lane at point marked * in written directions; on return take the field path from Shepherdsfield Lane direct to A64 and bus stops.

This walk is designed to be easily combined with a visit to Kirkham Priory, now owned and managed by English Heritage. This ruined Augustinian Priory, in a magnificent setting, dates from between the 12th and 14th centuries. As well as fine remains of the cloisters and church, of special interest are the medieval floor tiles, washbasins and magnificent decorated gatehouse. Open most days from Easter to October – details www.english-heritage.org.uk/visit/places/kirkham-priory, tel 01653 618768.

From the car park, walk downhill to cross the River Derwent at the fine old Kirkham Bridge – note the monastic fishponds on the right. Cross the railway level crossing. About 10 yards behind the crossing signal box take the brick steps on the right signed Whitwell. Follow this path alongside the railway for 220 yards. Bear left along a narrow but well defined path. Head steeply uphill towards woods and a farmhouse on the skyline.

Part way along this bumpy path are spectacular views across the railway and the thickly wooded valley known as the Kirkham Gorge. This great natural feature was created after the last Ice Age by flood water from the long-vanished Lake Pickering (now the Vale of Pickering) forcing its way through the soft clays between the chalk uplands of the Yorkshire Wolds and the Jurassic limestone Howardian Hills. This steep sided, winding gorge allows the River Derwent not to head as might be assumed to the Scarborough Coast, but southwards to join the Ouse below York. As you climb, there are increasingly splendid views along the gorge shared by the turbulent river and the York-Scarborough railway line. A Trans-Pennine train rushing through might add to the drama.

Head for the pedestrian gate above a deep ghyll, through another gate and stile. Bear left around the field edge. Then go half right to the farmhouse above at Bellmire Hill – also steep. Look for a waymarked gate between the farmhouse and the barn. Go through here and cross to Shepherdsfield Lane. Left here.

(Walkers heading for the A64 and Coastliner Bus should take the signed Welburn path, almost opposite, along

Yellow pimpernel

the hedge which leads via two stiles to the A64. Turn left for the bus stops.)

Follow the lane for 450 yards to the junction with Onhams Lane – a busy road so walk on the right to face direction of traffic. After 300 yards a pedestrian gate signed Crambe ¼ mile* leads to a fieldpath with a tall thorn hedge to your right. Follow this to a second gate by a copse. The path now curves around a long field. Gradually it descends to a third gate to cross a small beck and stile. Keep the same direction downhill. Bear right at the bottom of the field to a track leading into the village of Crambe. Keep ahead to the village centre and church.

Crambe is an attractive ridge top village with an especially lovely church, which an early Norman tower and

Woodsage

chancel. Just before the church, note the tiny schoolroom, now a private house, built for the village by Colonel Chumley in 1844. Look out for the amazing gargoyle in the south wall of the church.

Take the path marked by a small gate, through the south of the churchyard between the graves. A pedestrian gate in the churchyard corner has a reassuring waymark. This leads to a path along the field edge which descends to the lane behind the village. Turn right here and follow this quiet lane for 400 yards. Where it turns sharp right, take the track left (signed Kirkham) which heads towards Oakcliffe Farm. Where the metalled track turns right towards the farmhouse, your path is straight ahead. Head up the grassland to the edge of Oakcliffe Wood. Turn right for 100 yards to the gate on the left leading into the wood.

This is a lovely section of narrow path through beech and pine woods, above the steep Derwent escarpment. When it emerges in an open field, the elegant spire of Welburn Church is a landmark.

Follow the path until it reaches the lane from Cramble at a farm gate and gap. Turn right for 30 yards to where another path (right) leads between a fence and wood. This enters the wood and soon descends steeply downhill. Care is required here as in winter or wet weather it can be extremely slippery – side paths may offer more grip. This path emerges at the main road. Turn right for the level crossing and Kirkham Priory.

Walk 6 – Temple of Four Winds & Mausoleum

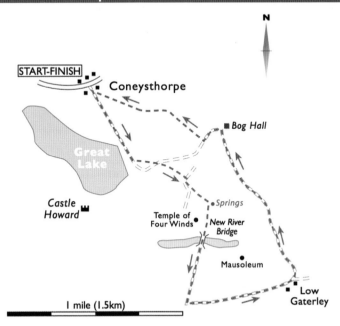

Distance: 5 miles (8 km). Time: 3 hours.
Terrain: Easy; mainly tracks and woodland or field paths, no stiles.
Start & finish: Coneysthorpe village (grid ref 713714).
Parking: Village Hall – please make payment at honesty box as requested.
Refreshments/facilities: None in village. Toilets at Malton, Castle Howard.
Public transport: Weekdays only, Stephensons 180/182 (walk can also be
easily accessed from Castle Howard – 1 mile – for more regular 181 and
summer Sunday services).

This spectacular walk on public rights of way through part of the Castle Howard Estate can be combined with a visit to Castle Howard itself, with all its visitor facilities. Throughout the walk there are wonderful views of the astonishing 18th-century landscape with architectural features that add so much to the house's setting.

The walk starts in the lovely little village of Coneysthorpe, with its early 19th-century Georgian chapel, recently restored, and extensive village green – a good place for a picnic.

Facing south, turn left from the green alongside the high estate wall in the direction of Malton. After 150 yards, you reach a narrow white gateway which gives pedestrian entrance to the park. Follow the signed path to Welburn. This soon joins a track heading south-west, following a line of trees below the lake. There are intriguing glimpses above and between the trees of the great dome of Castle Howard.

After around 800 yards, you reach a woodland on the right. The right of way (not clear on the ground) branches left by the trees along the field edge. If you miss the turn, continue to the junction of tracks ahead. Turn left for 120 yards, to the large footpath sign (719705). Turn right here along a narrow, somewhat overgrown path that winds through scrubby woodland known as Horse Close Rush before joining another track. Keep right as it leads into open pasture. Where it swings right, maintain the same direction to an area of enclosed, marshy springs ahead. Another tall footpath sign (724704) indicates the line of a footpath to the right, heading due south through open pastureland and climbing a low hill.

You are soon opposite the Temple of Four Winds – a beautiful, elegant classical temple designed by the great architect of Castle Howard, John Vanbrugh. Each façade faces a different direction – hence the name Four Winds.

Primroses and violets

As you continue up the gentle rise, on the left is another architectural masterpiece, Nicholas Hawksmoor's magnificent Mausoleum, last resting place of the Earls of Carlisle. The Temple of Four Winds and Mausoleum in their great landscape setting have been described as two of the finest small buildings in England. Note, too, another remarkable landscape feature – a stone pyramid on the low ridge across fields to your right, reflecting an 18th-century obsession with all things Egyptian.

Heron

Keep the same direction over the brow of the hill. Descend and cross the large stone bridge below and ahead. New Bridge is a lovely ornamental bridge over a narrow lake, created, like Castle Howard's Great Lake, by dams and sluices on small local becks to create a shimmering water feature purely for landscape effect.

Keep ahead on the green track between fields to a junction with a surfaced farm access track. Turn left along what is now the Centenary Way, signed Hutton Ambo. You are now walking to the south and east of the Mausoleum, with wonderful views of this classical structure from different angles. As you walk there are intriguing glimpses of Castle Howard's baroque dome.

The track heads east, past Lowdy Hill Gill farm. Look for the path 180 yards beyond, signed Coneysthorpe, a stony track. After another 100 yards, and opposite large barns at Low Gaterley, take the track, waymarked, left.

This curves its way behind the Mausoleum before heading north to a small woodland. It then crosses a bridge over the beck. Then go north-west to Bog Hall, which despite its name is an attractive farm. The track winds between farm buildings. Bear left where you reach the bridge over Mill Hills Beck. Do not cross the bridge but take the waymarked path right, before the bridge (not as shown on current OS maps). This follows the field edge to the eastside of the beck. It heads around the outside of the Collier Hag Plantation before bearing left to a gate – again waymarked. Go through here.

Cross a narrow field to the next gate. Keep heading north-west over pasture. Look straight ahead and you will see the white narrow pedestrian gate and track where the walk began. Look for the marked gap in the electric fence ahead. Turn left at the gate to walk along the lane back to Coneysthorpe.

Walk 7 – Welburn, Four Faces and the Pyramid

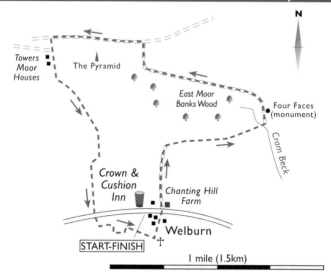

Distance: 4 miles (6.5 km). Time: 2 hours.
Terrain: Easy; mainly tracks, field paths, one stile.
Start & finish: Welburn village (grid ref 721680).
Parking: along Main Street – avoid causing obstruction or blocking entrances.
Refreshments/facilities: Crown & Cushion Inn; Leaf & Loaf bakery and café.
Toilets in village hall.
Public transport: Stephensons 182 from Malton.

Like Walk 6, this easy, circular walk through Castle Howard estate is designed to experience several great architectural features in their spectacular landscape setting. Welburn is a long, linear village of cream coloured stone cottages and houses with red pantile roofs and attractive gardens, and a handsome parish church.

From the Crown and Cushion, walk 100 yards eastwards towards Malton. Turn at the evocatively named Chanting Hill farmhouse to descend Water Lane, a cul-de-sac. At the entrance to Primrose Hill house, fork left along the track between the house and a field.

At the crossing of paths, turn right. The bridleway is signed slightly misleadingly to Welburn. It follows a green track alongside field and hedge. This gradually descends and narrows to a path through dense woodland in a shallow valley. At a junction turn left on the track signed to Coneysthorpe. This goes through a stile with an adjacent gap. It then bears right, over a footbridge across Moorhouse Beck. Head left up the side of the valley on a track. You reach another track and crossing in Pretty Wood. Take the signed track to the left marked Centenary Way.

Before doing so, look back and to your right among the trees to see a tall, ornately carved ornamental pillar, Les Quatre Visages, or Four Faces. As its name implies, there are four grimacing faces, three smiling, one more serious; a handsome if mysterious folly hidden deep in the woods.

Follow the gently ascending track heading north-west above East Moor Banks. After half a mile, at a gate, the track swings right, now signed Coneysthorpe, to leave the wood. As you cross open fields there is a magnificent view of the Hawksmoor Mausoleum on your right, on its low hillock, in a spectacular setting.

At the T-junction, turn left along the farm access lane. You cross part of Walk 6, but this time keep the same westerly direction, signed Bulmer, soon passing the Pyramid on the left. Another amazing feature, this was built in 1728 as a memorial to Lord William Howard, the founder of Castle Howard and scion of the family, who died in 1639. Just beyond is another striking folly, this time a mock medieval castle turret, complete with arrow slits and a long stretch of ornamental wall that culminates in a contrasting octagonal tower.

Almost opposite the first turret, a narrow path, signed Welburn, crosses the fields then heads downhill on a grassy surface. Follow the waymarks towards Moor Houses Farm. At the farm take the

kissing gate covered with unusual wooden palings. Turn left between farm buildings to an identical gate on the left. Follow this around the outside of the farm to a third gate. Head alongside a wire fence then hedge, with fine views to the rear of the Pyramid.

At the fourth identical gate, the path bears right along a thorn hedge to yet another pedestrian gate in the dip. Keep ahead to the only stile on the walk. This leads into a huge field. Turn sharp right here, around the field edge. The path, well defined, crosses a large arable field. Welburn church spire is a useful orientation ahead. At a crossing of paths (718685) turn right to the next field gap and hedge. Turn left. The waymarked path soon passes farm buildings. Follow the pedestrian way to the right of the farm access track, to the edge of Welburn village. Turn left here.

Woodsage

If wanting to avoid road walking into the village, take the first opening on the right (716680). This leads to a house. Bear left on a track which becomes an attractive footpath behind gardens. At the school car park gate, take the narrow enclosed path, waymarked, on the right. After 50 yards turn left behind and around the school playground. Turn left again, then right, to head behind more gardens towards the mid-Victorian church – a handsome neo-Gothic structure.

From the church, turn left along the lane. Keep directly ahead, past the village hall to Welburn centre and its welcoming café and pub.

Walk 8 – Hovingham Park and South Wood

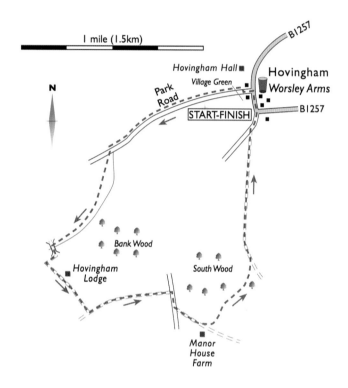

I mile (1.5km)

B1257

Hovingham Hall ■
Village Green

Hovingham
Worsley Arms

N

Park
Road

START-FINISH

B1257

Bank Wood

South Wood

Hovingham
Lodge

Manor
House
Farm

Distance: 4½ miles (7 km). Time: 2¼ hours.
Terrain: Fairly easy; mainly woodland tracks and field paths, but with several
stiles, and a couple of moderate ascents.
Start & finish: Hovingham village (grid ref 667757).
Parking: Alongside the village green – avoid causing obstruction or blocking
entrances. Small car park at the end of Park Lane by the stone gateway.
Refreshments/facilities: Worsley Arms (bar in rear of hotel); Malt Shovel Inn;
Hovingham Bakery and Spa Tea room. Toilets in inns and café, customers only.
Public transport: Stephensons 194 from Malton or Helmsley (connections
from York at Helmsley).

Mallards

This walk starts and finishes in the beautiful village of Hovingham, dominated by the magnificent entrance to Hovingham Hall and Park. There is an extensive village green, red pantiles and cream stone cottages, plus a fine Victorian church. Hovingham Hall, a superb Georgian house, has been the ancestral home of the Worsleys, one of Yorkshire's great land-owning families since the 16th century. It was the childhood home of the present Duchess of Kent. The hall is only open to the public during June – details www.hovingham.co.uk tel 01653 628771.

Most of this walk lies within part of the Hovingham Estate (please keep all dogs on leads), starting with a beautiful permissive route through the edge of the park. You follow a shallow, wooded valley around Bank Wood, and return to Hovingham through South Wood and a stretch of the Ebor Way, including memorable views across the Vale of Pickering.

Start the walk at the village green opposite the Worsley Arms. Facing south, turn right along Park Street. Head between the stone gateway pillars, then alongside the park wall (take care: keep single file and walk on the right to face fast moving approaching traffic) for 100 yards to a stile by a gate on the right (666756). Keep left immediately over another stile.

This leads to a permissive path through the park. Keep left alongside the fence for 350 yards to a crossing path with an ornamental stone bridge on your right. Cross the bridge but keep sharp left along the streamside, then the roadside hedge. You reach another gate and stile into the road. Cross with care.

Directly opposite is a track carrying a

footpath signed to Coulton. This leads to a gate to dense woodland. The path narrows through lush vegetation. Keep ahead to a stile. The path enters rough pastureland. Keep alongside the stream, across a stile and wooden footbridge. Stay in the same direction to a kissing gate leading into a track.

Turn left (649744) along a cindery track over the bridge (signed Scackleton). Follow this track uphill, bearing left and then right past the cottage. Curve left up to a finger post. Keep straight ahead here, still signed for Scackleton. Pass the old stables and fine buildings of Hovingham Lodge. Continue up to another junction of tracks. Turn left here for 650 yards on a green track alongside a large arable field. This descends to a dip before climbing to the busy Hovingham road.

Turn right. Walk for 150 yards on the broad verge on the right. Cross to enter the farm track (660738) leading towards Aireyholme Farm. Continue to the first farm, Moorhouse, past the outbuildings and farmhouse. Opposite a fine pantiled barn, look for the waymarked post indicating a well-defined footpath across the field on the left.

This leads to a gate into woodland. Beyond this gate a track climbs into

Hazel

South Wood. Continue for 300 yards to where the path enters a newly cleared area, and bears left (signed). Keep ahead, as the track merges with another, now signed the Ebor Way. Alongside arable fields, the path emerges at the crest of the hill.

There are magnificent views from here as you descend. You are looking across the green and fertile Vale of Pickering spread out below. In the distance is the line of hills forming the southern edge of the high tableland of the North York Moors National Park. Further down, the pretty, red pantiled rooftops of Hovingham come into view.

Follow the track as it descends to join the Terrington road just above Hovingham. Keep straight ahead downhill. As you approach Hovingham, look for the little stepped footpath on the left that cuts the corner and leads directly into Hovingham High Street.

Dragonfly

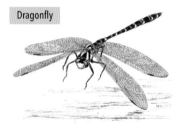

Walk 9 – Slingsby Heights

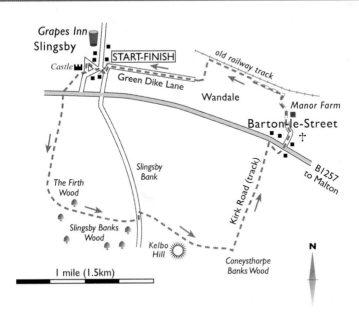

Distance: 6 miles (9.5 km). Time: 3 hours.
Terrain: Easy; mainly tracks; one gentle climb.
Start & finish: Slingsby Green (grid ref 698749).
Parking: Ample on-road parking along The Green or on Railway Street.
Please park carefully so as not to cause obstruction.
Refreshments/facilities: Grapes Inn on Railway Street; local bakery shop on
Green Dike Lane. Toilets in village pub for customers only.
Public transport: Weekdays only. Stephensons 194 Malton-Hovingham
(connections from York at Helmsley).

This walk takes advantage of and follows the low hill ridge between Castle Howard Estate and the Vale of Pickering. On offer are fine views as far as the North York Moors, and also south to the rolling hills, scattered woodland and carefully landscaped vistas around Castle Howard itself. Slingsby is an attractive village, with a ruined castle which was once a grand Jacobean house (strictly no access to the ruins which are in a dangerous state), a handsome Victorian church and popular village pub.

From the village green head due west towards Slingsby Castle. Turn left into High Street. After 50 yards, look for the signed footpath right, leading into a concrete farm yard. Head for the pedestrian gate in the right corner of the yard. Through here, take the path diagonally left signed to Malton Road. This crosses three small horse paddocks, through pedestrian gates, to emerge at a stile on the B1257 Malton Road.

Cross with care, taking the broad farm track, a bridleway, directly ahead, signed Firth Wood. Keep straight ahead on what is a gentle climb for half a mile. The track twists past a barn and climbs up the ridge. There are increasingly impressive views behind you back across Slingsby itself and the Vale of Pickering as you ascend.

Redpoll

The track enters Firth Wood, with its cypress and sycamore trees. It becomes a much narrower path, though still a bridleway, curving to the left between the trees. It then becomes a narrower, grassy way. Turn left at the meeting with another track where signposts indicate Centenary Way and Coneysthorpe.

Follow the long ridge, with views across the Vale of Pickering to the left, and through the trees towards Castle Howard. Where the track descends to the road up Slingsby Bank, the woodland opens out. Cross the road, taking the path through the gate ahead which curves along a grassy bank.

There are superb views from here (704732) along the tree-lined road that forms the grand avenue and entrance to Castle Howard. The stone gateway entrance is in the middle distance and beyond it on the skyline the 110ft high Memorial Column to the Earl of Carlisle.

The path enters the woodlands above Kelbro Hill at another gate. (This woodland was due to be felled during 2016 – if this is happening follow the warning notices and any temporary

Tawny owl

diversion signs.) Continue past the point where the Coneysthorpe bridleway turns off right, to where another bridle gate, left, indicates the way to Barton-le-Street (717729). This is Kirk Road, an ancient track alongside a long arable field. Panoramic views from here across the Vale include the town of Pickering to the north and even the adventure rides at Flamingo Land theme park.

Follow the track as it descends the field and curves sharp right to emerge on the B1257. Cross with care to the lane to the centre of Barton-le-Street. Take time to discover Barton's little church on your right. There was a medieval church on the site which was demolished and totally rebuilt in the 19th century, but several remarkable medieval carvings were retained and incorporated into the fabric of the newer church, particularly around the porch.

Keep ahead to the village green. Take the surfaced way left across the green. Follow the signs towards Slingsby into Manor Farm, where a helpful red sign indicates the public path ahead. Go left behind farm buildings. Bear left, then right, into a broad farm track between fences, heading due north out of Barton. Go around two bends, but where a line of wooden electric pylons crosses the track, look for the little Slingsby FP sign (719748) on the left. This indicates the grass path alongside the pylons between arable fields. Take the path to a hedge. Follow the blue bridleway signs right and then left alongside the remains of an old fence and scrubby land.

These earthworks and scraps of fence are all that remains of the former Malton-Hovingham-Thirsk Railway, a winding, single track country line through Ryedale. It opened in 1853 but closed to passengers in 1930 and to goods in 1964, even before Dr Beeching's axe. The sharp eyed might spot the former crossing keeper's cottage at Long Lane.

Keep the same direction past the crossing path from Wansdale farm. Head left of, and alongside, the old railway trackbed to emerge at Long Lane (710751). Turn left here to the surfaced end of Green Dyke Lane. Go right along this quiet lane, past Melgate House and the cemetery, to Slingsby.

Bog asphodel

Walk 10 – Terrington – a Touch of Tuscany

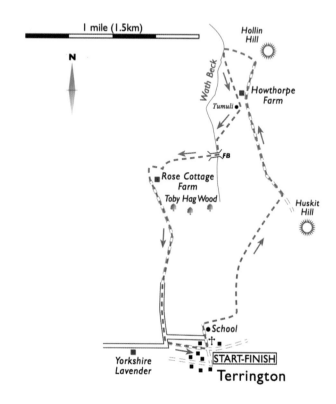

I mile (1.5km)

N

Hollin Hill

Wath Beck

Howthorpe Farm

Tumuli

FB

Rose Cottage Farm

Toby Hag Wood

Huskit Hill

School

Yorkshire Lavender

START-FINISH

Terrington

Distance: 4½ miles (7 km). Time: 2 hours.
Terrain: Moderate – tracks and field paths, but with several fairly steep climbs and one area of damp ground to negotiate – boots essential.
Start & finish: Terrington village (grid ref 672707).
Parking: In Church Street by the church off the main road; if busy, in The Square. Please avoid causing obstruction or blocking entrances.
Refreshments/facilities: Village store and tea room; also at Yorkshire Lavender Farm. Toilets in village hall (except when events are taking place there) and at cafés for customers only. Village pub due to open in 2016.
Public transport: Stephensons 180 (infrequent) from York or Malton.

Terrington has much of the feeling and atmosphere of a Tuscan hill village, situated as it is at the end of a low ridge in lush, fertile but surprisingly hilly countryside, with extensive views. It has a lovely old church with a part Saxon tower, an attractive tree covered village green, and just to the west, the beautifully located Yorkshire Lavender Farm, a visit to which can easily be combined with this walk.

Walk up Church Lane past the church. Keep directly ahead at the end of the lane. Follow the Centenary Way waymarks into a grassy path alongside and between a stone walk and Terrington Hall School. This path goes through a gate into the parking area for the school playing fields. Take the path signed Ebor Way, turning sharp right. Follow the path alongside the rugby field and descend along the edge of an arable field.

At the field corner (674709) turn left on the broad, grassy path along the headland beside the hedge. Go through two metal gates (waymarked) before a steepish climb up the side of Huskit Hill.

Red bunting; left, fly agaric

You reach a stone track signed Ebor and Centenary Way.

Turn left. Follow the track uphill, along and over the ridge to the entrance of Howthorpe Farm. Go through the farm gate. Turn sharp right. Follow the footpath sign to avoid the farmyard, and pick up the track to the right hand side of the farm. This descends into a shallow valley.

Turn left immediately before the bridge over the stream. Head along the bridleway and stream by Hollin Hill Wood for 300 yards, through a gate. Take the path (signed) to the left before the next gate, alongside a shallow stream, Wath Beck, and a narrow wood. The right of way veers to the left away from the rather boggy streamside over some mysterious grass covered formations.

These earthworks are possibly some kind of ancient defensive structures linked to nearby tumuli, perhaps Bronze Age in origin, shown on the OS map (675728) just below Howthorpe Farm.

Head left, climbing steeply towards the trees on the skyline just to the north of Howthorpe Farm. Through the gate into the farmyard head for the stile in the fence to the right. (This is close to the gateway reached earlier – a way of shortening the walk.) The stile leads to a path which descends steeply, diagonally half right, towards the long hedge opposite. Locate a stile to access the next field. Continue to the next stile in the bottom right hand corner by the wood and stream below.

A tricky section now follows, as in winter or after rain, this section of streamside path, though attractive, can be extremely boggy. If so, head a few yards to the left, to the edge of the grassy slope above the rank rushes. Go along the edge of the boggy area for 150 yards to cross back over to where a wooden pedestrian gate leads over a small footbridge over Wath Beck (675725). Go through the gate straight ahead.

Now follow a steep path up the hillside, alongside fence and hedge past Toby Hag Wood, the copse to your left. There are fine views back across the valley to your right. At the summit of the ridge, keep straight ahead through the gate (waymarked).

The path alongside the fence bears left down towards Rose Cottage Farm. As you approach the farm, follow the waymarks directing you right into a narrow path between fences. This continues outside the farm enclosures, then left alongside and parallel to the farm access lane. It joins the lane just above Sawmill Cottage and a pond hidden by trees.

Your route now ascends to join the surfaced lane of New Road. With Cotril Farm to the left, the lane emerges at the end of Torrington village at Mill Hill. If you are visiting Yorkshire Lavender, the entrance is 250 yards to your right, down the lane.

The 60-acre Yorkshire Lavender Farm (www.yorkshirelavender.com tel 01653 648008) is open daily between March and October. There are extensive gardens and lavender beds, a tea room, shop plus magnificent panoramic views across the Vale of York. Entry free.

To return to Terrington village, turn sharp left down the back lane which runs behind the village to enjoy lovely views of the pantiled roofs and church tower.

Fallow deer